Coloring Book Love
Mandalas
Volume 2

K.S. PIERCE

Copyright © 2015 by K.S. Pierce and Coloring Book Love, www.ColoringBookLove.com

All rights reserved. Printed in the United States of America

ISBN: 978-0-692-51835-9
First Edition: August 2015

SHARE YOUR CREATIONS WITH US!

Welcome to the Coloring Book Love Mandalas Volume 2!

In this volume, I encourage you to turn the pages and start your coloring journey with 60 Mandalas with varying shapes and patterns. This coloring book showcases both hand-drawn and computer generated images. Go on a creative adventure and start your relaxation, meditation, manifestation, creative expression, inspiration, self-discovery and healing all from the comfort of your favorite corner or spot to color.

Mandalas represent wholeness and are perfect for decorating with all kinds of mediums - color pencils, crayons, markers, gel pens, or watercolors, among others.

Coloring these Mandalas is a unique method of visual self expression. You may experience a feeling of relief, a sense of peace as the pattern comes together within the circle. They are not only beautiful with intricate patterns or designs, they are also powerful tools for inspiration, self-discovery and healing.

It is my ardent hope that as you flip through the pages of this coloring book and start coloring you find yourself being freed from whatever worries, stresses or negativities pulling you down. It's about time. You deserve it.

Happy coloring!
K.S. Pierce

You're never too old (or too young) to color!

Here's what to do next:

1. Find a comfortable place where you can color. This coloring book is created precisely so you can enjoy the process.

2. If you would like to make several versions of your artwork, or are afraid you might make mistakes, make sure to make a copy of the page. This will also give you the chance to select your preferred paper (thicker and won't bleed) ready for framing.

3. Please note that if you are using markers or gel pens, consider using scrap paper behind the page you're coloring to prevent bleed-through.

4. Use your favorite medium or a combination of mediums. Break out your favorite coloring pencils, coloring markers, gel pens, crayons, etc., and start your coloring journey!

5. Most important of all - Be yourself, express yourself! Remember, there is no wrong way, or right way to paint or color. Whatever you decide to do with these pages, the result will be unique and beautiful!

6. Once you're done with your creations, share them with the world! You may display them or give them as gifts.

7. It's time for your relaxation, meditation, manifestation, creative expression, inspiration, self-discovery and healing. Let's begin!

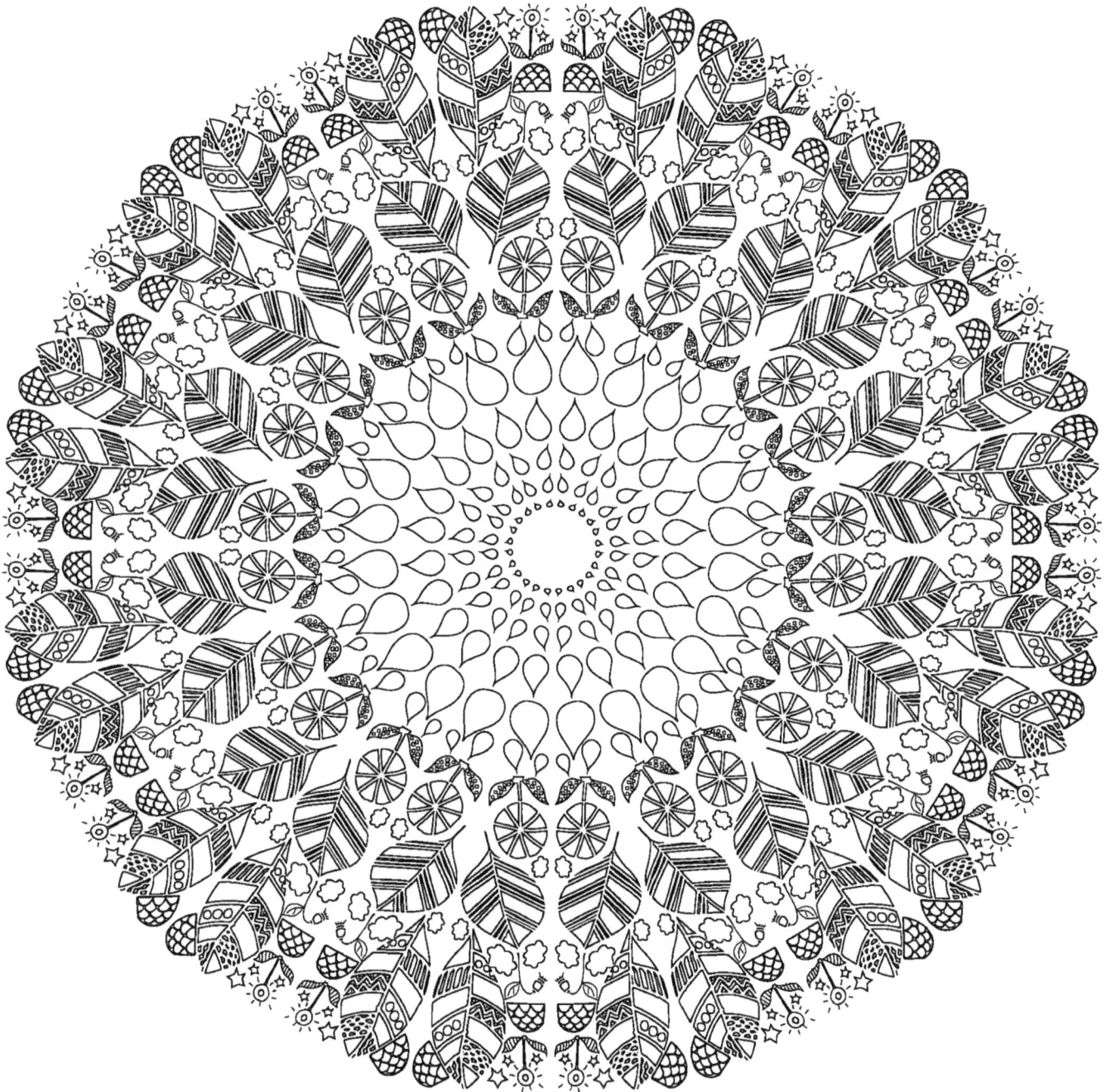

Love takes off masks that we fear we cannot live without
and know we cannot live within.

— James Baldwin

Love yourself first and everything else falls into line.
You really have to love yourself
to get anything done in this world.
– Lucille Ball

Once the realization is accepted
that even between the closest human beings
infinite distances continue,
a wonderful living side by side can grow,
if they succeed in loving the distance between them
which makes it possible for each
to see the other whole against the sky.
- Rainer Maria Rilke

The most important thing in life
is to learn how to give out love,
and to let it come in.
- Morrie Schwartz

If I know what love is, it is because of you.
- Herman Hesse

I love you not because of who you are,
but because of who I am when I am with you.
- Roy Croft

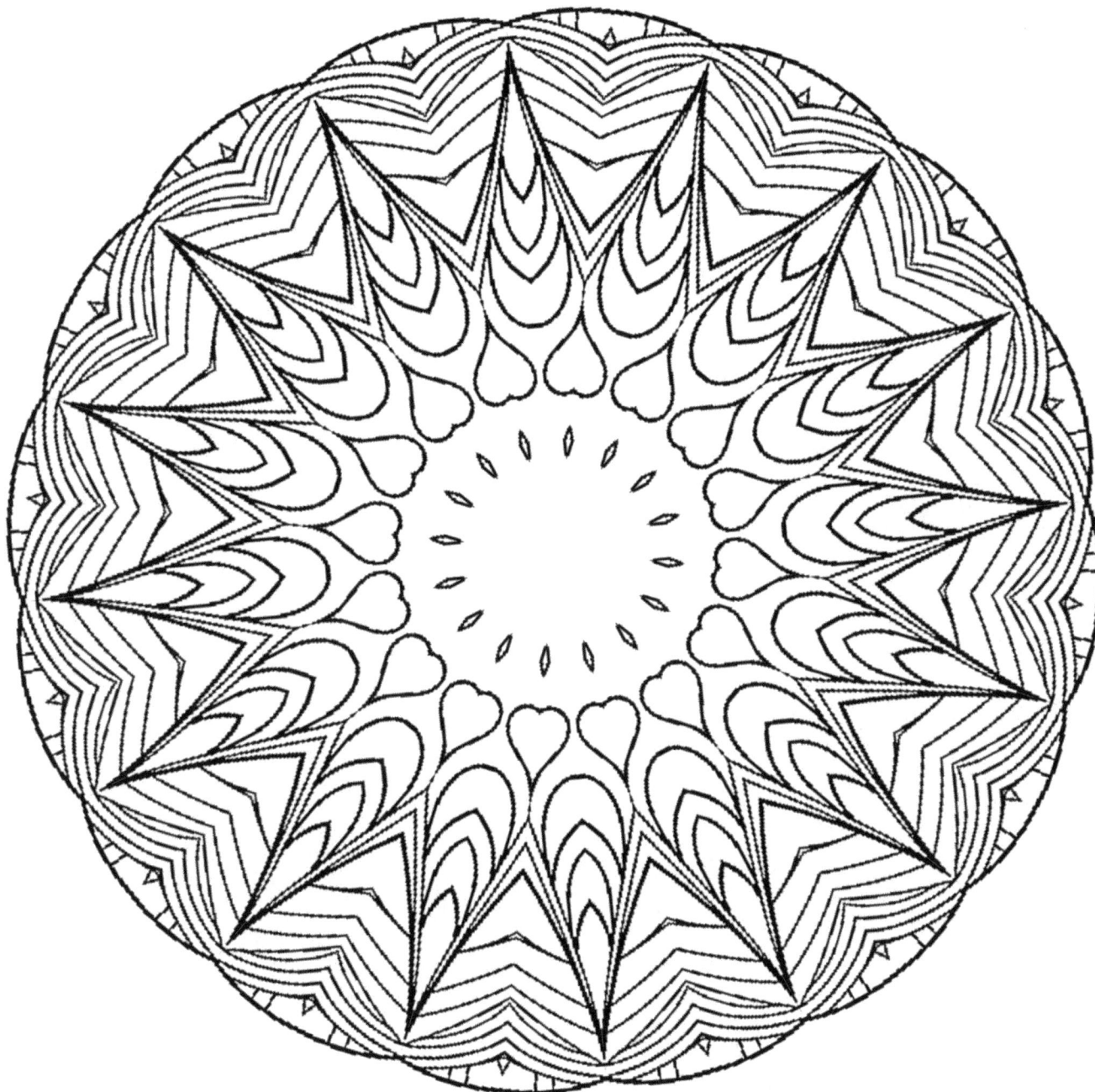

We are shaped and fashioned by what we love.
- Johann Wolfgang von Goethe

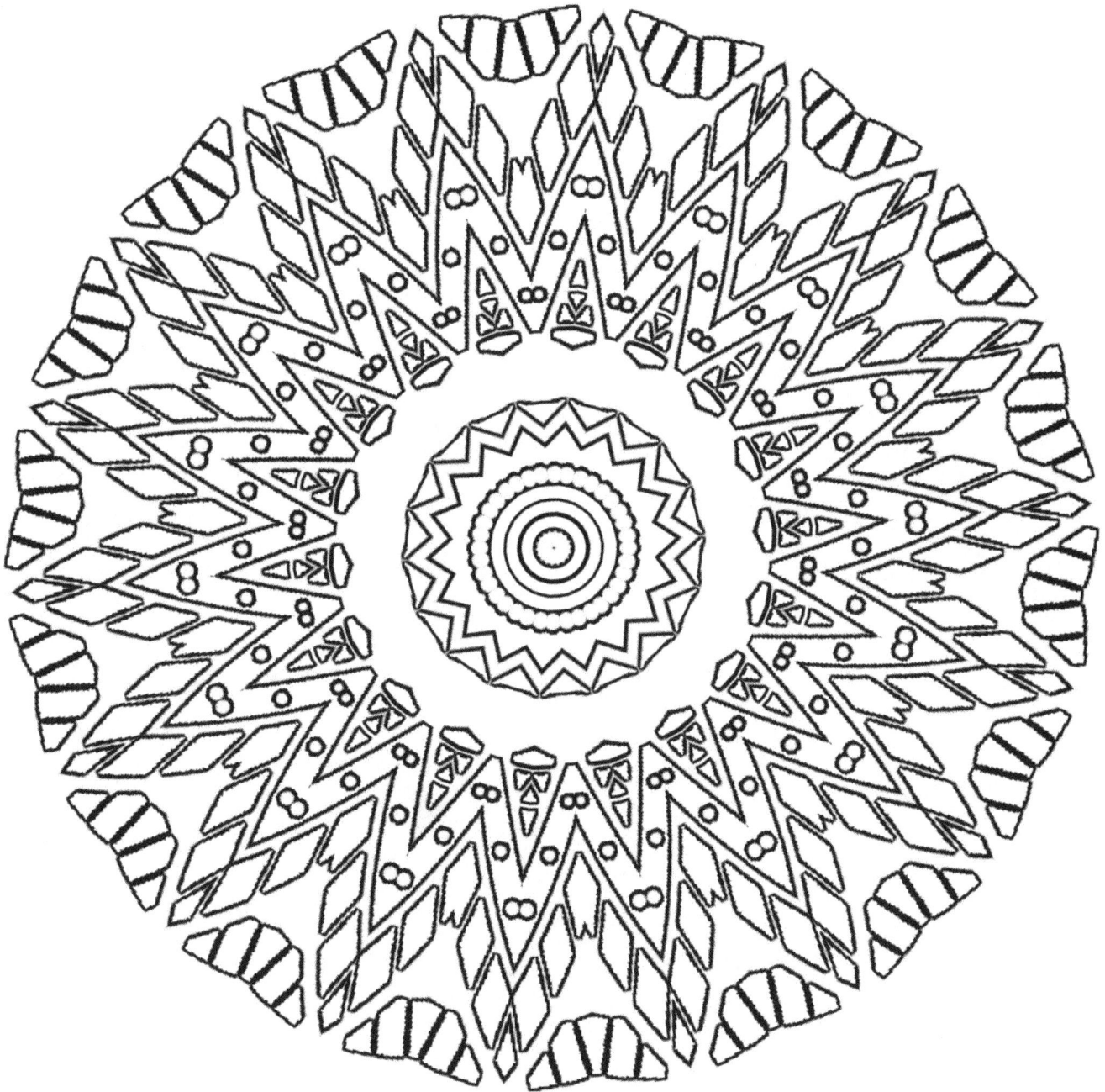

When we are in love
we seem to ourselves quite different
from what we were before.
- Blaise Pascal

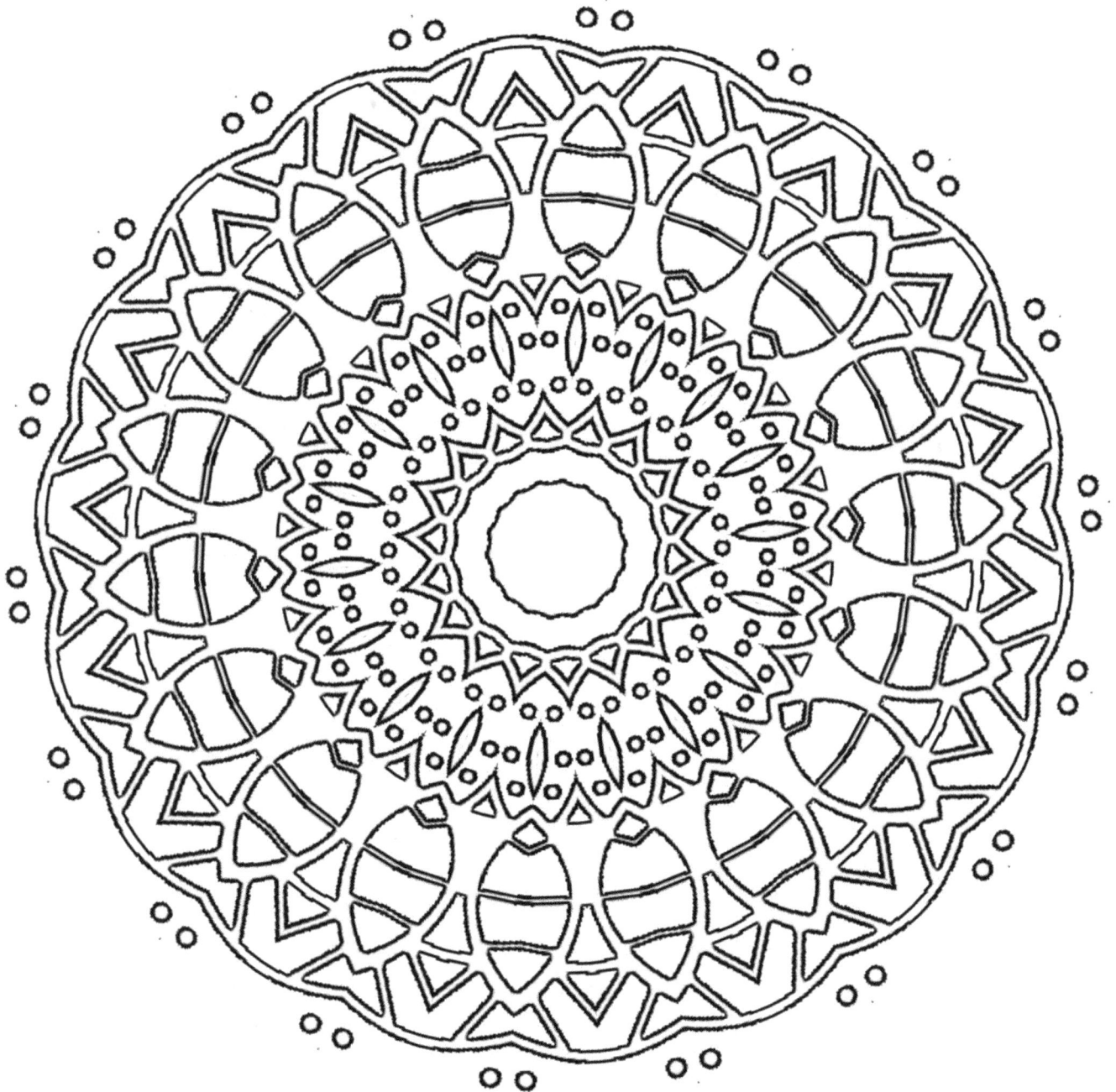

It takes courage to love,
but pain through love is the purifying fire
which those who love generously know.
We all know people who are so much afraid of pain
that they shut themselves up like clams in a shell and,
giving out nothing, receive nothing and therefore shrink
until life is a mere living death.
- Eleanor Roosevelt

Don't brood.
Get on with living and loving.
You don't have forever.
- Leo Buscaglia

Your task is not to seek for love,
but merely to seek and find
all the barriers within yourself
that you have built against it.
– Rumi

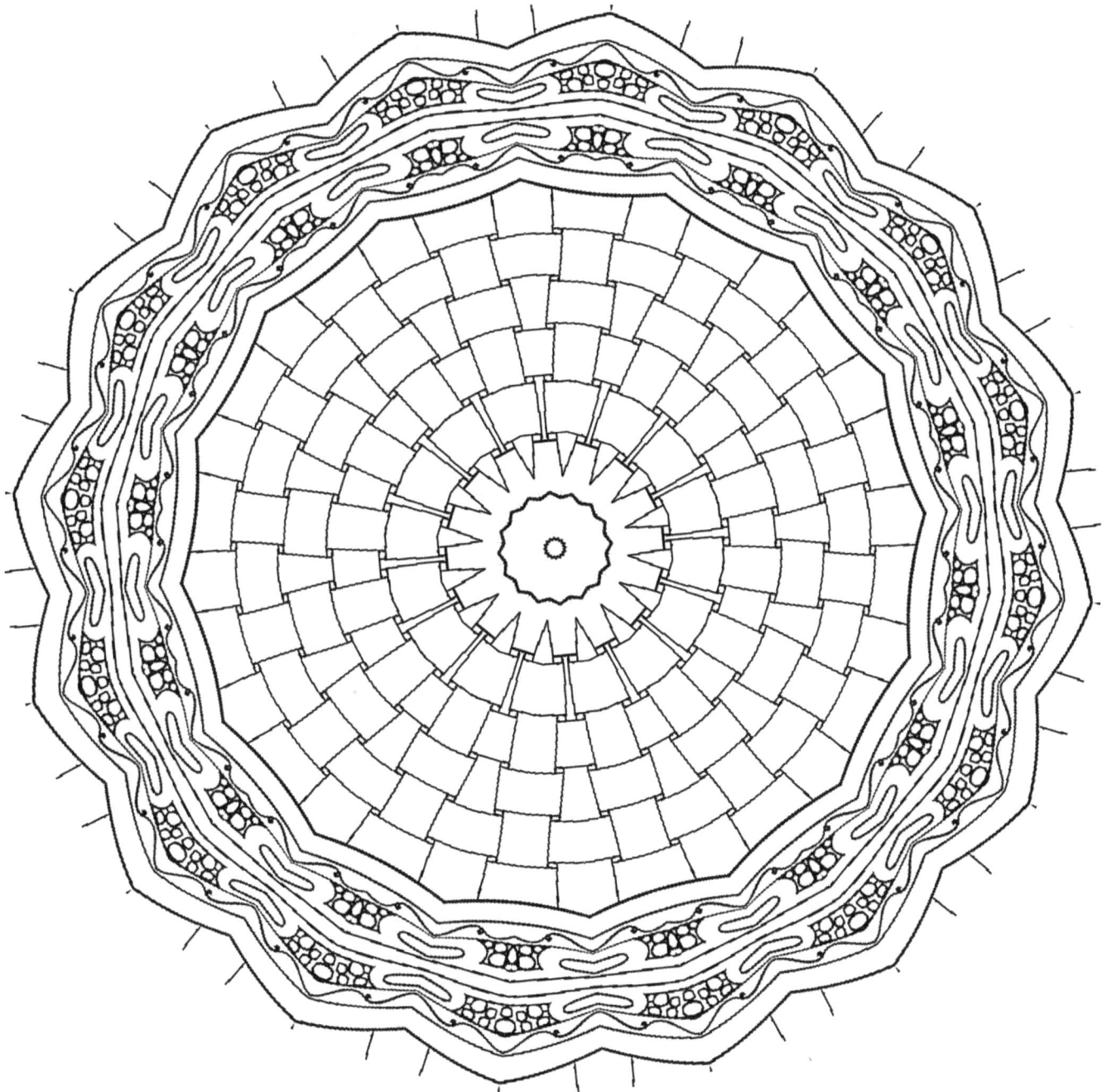

Love is of all passions the strongest,
for it attacks simultaneously
the head, the heart and the senses.
- Lao Tzu

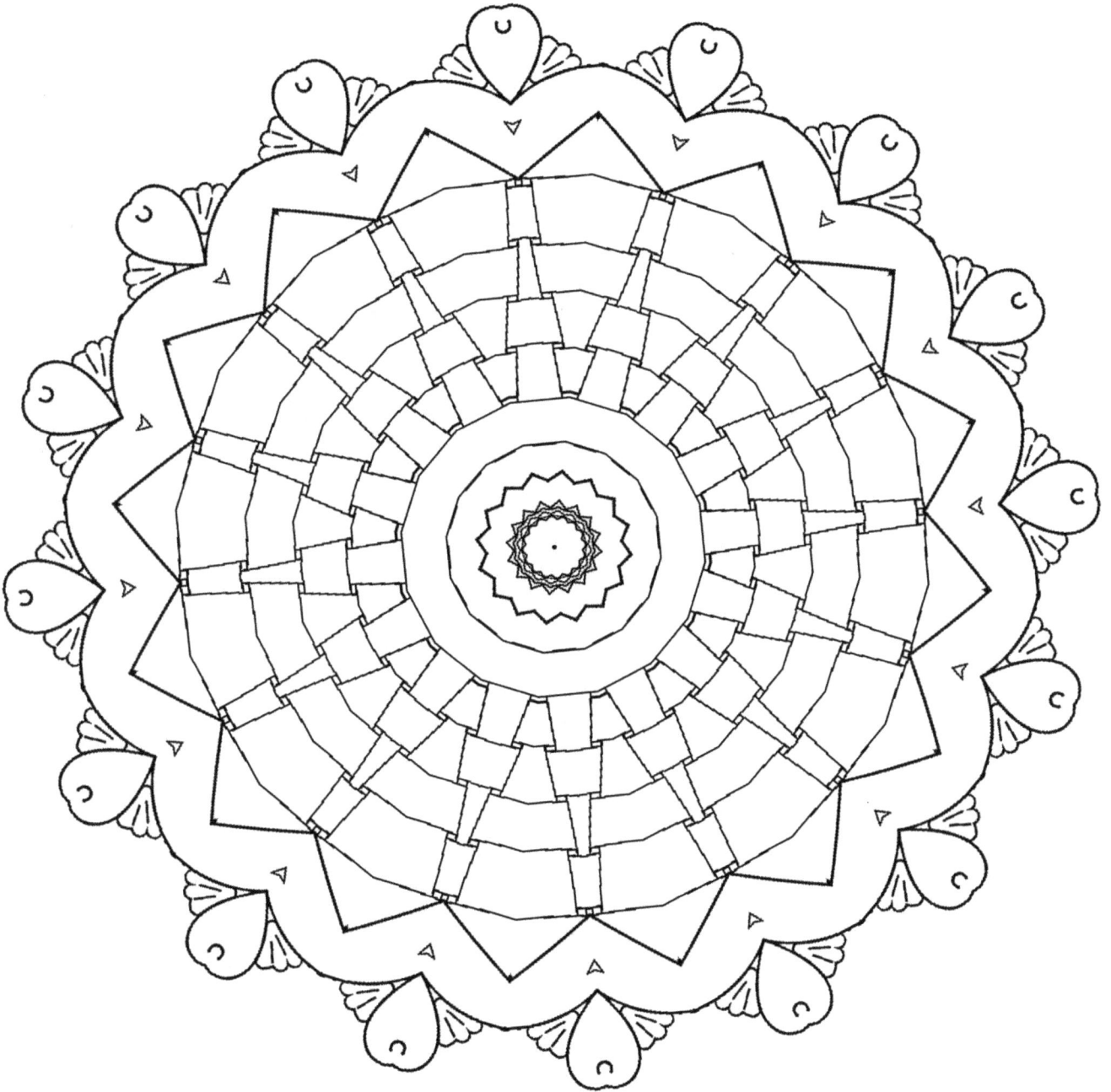

You know it's love
when all you want is that person to be happy,
even if you're not part of their happiness.
- Julia Roberts

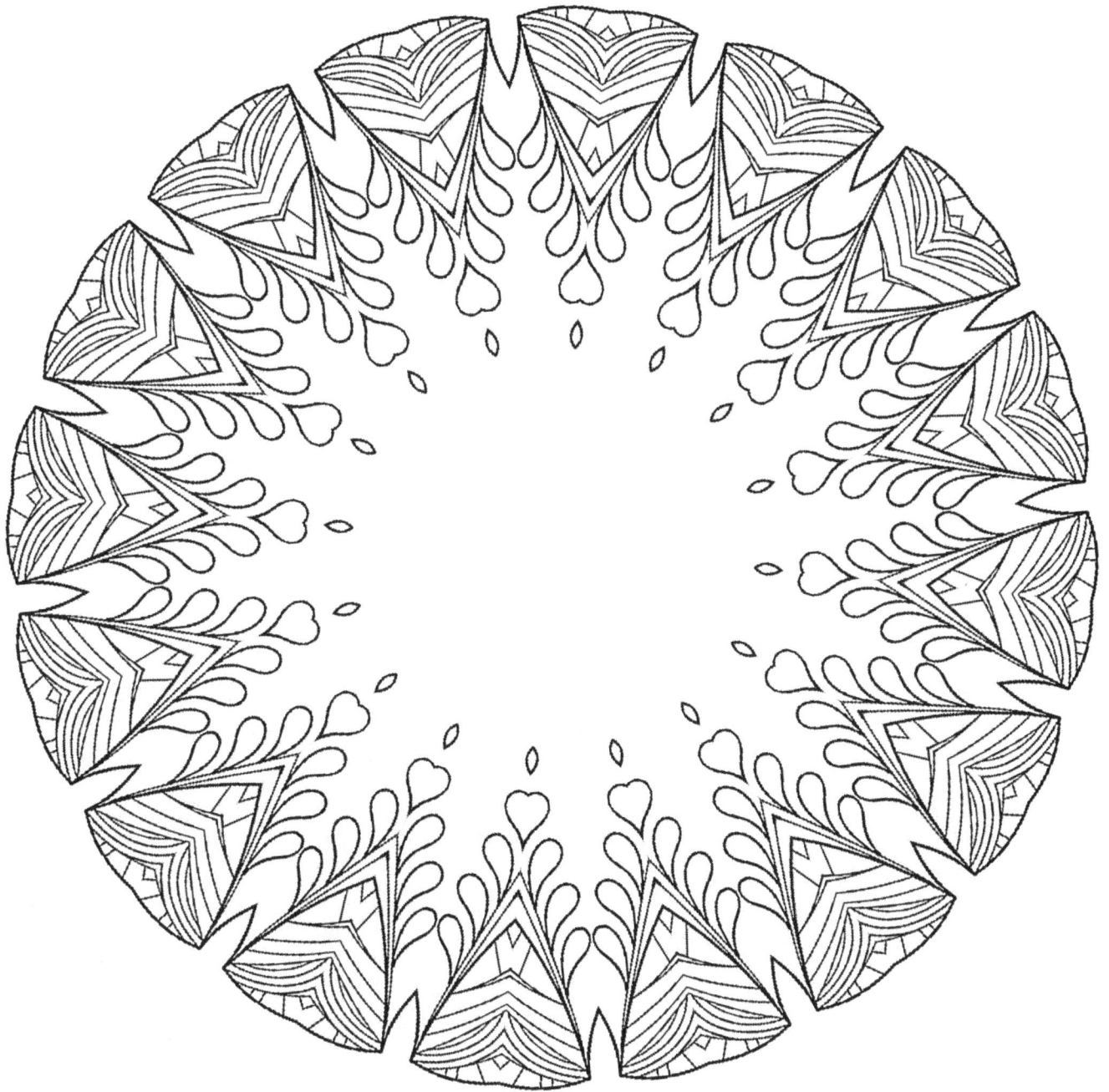

At the touch of love everyone becomes a poet.
 - Plato

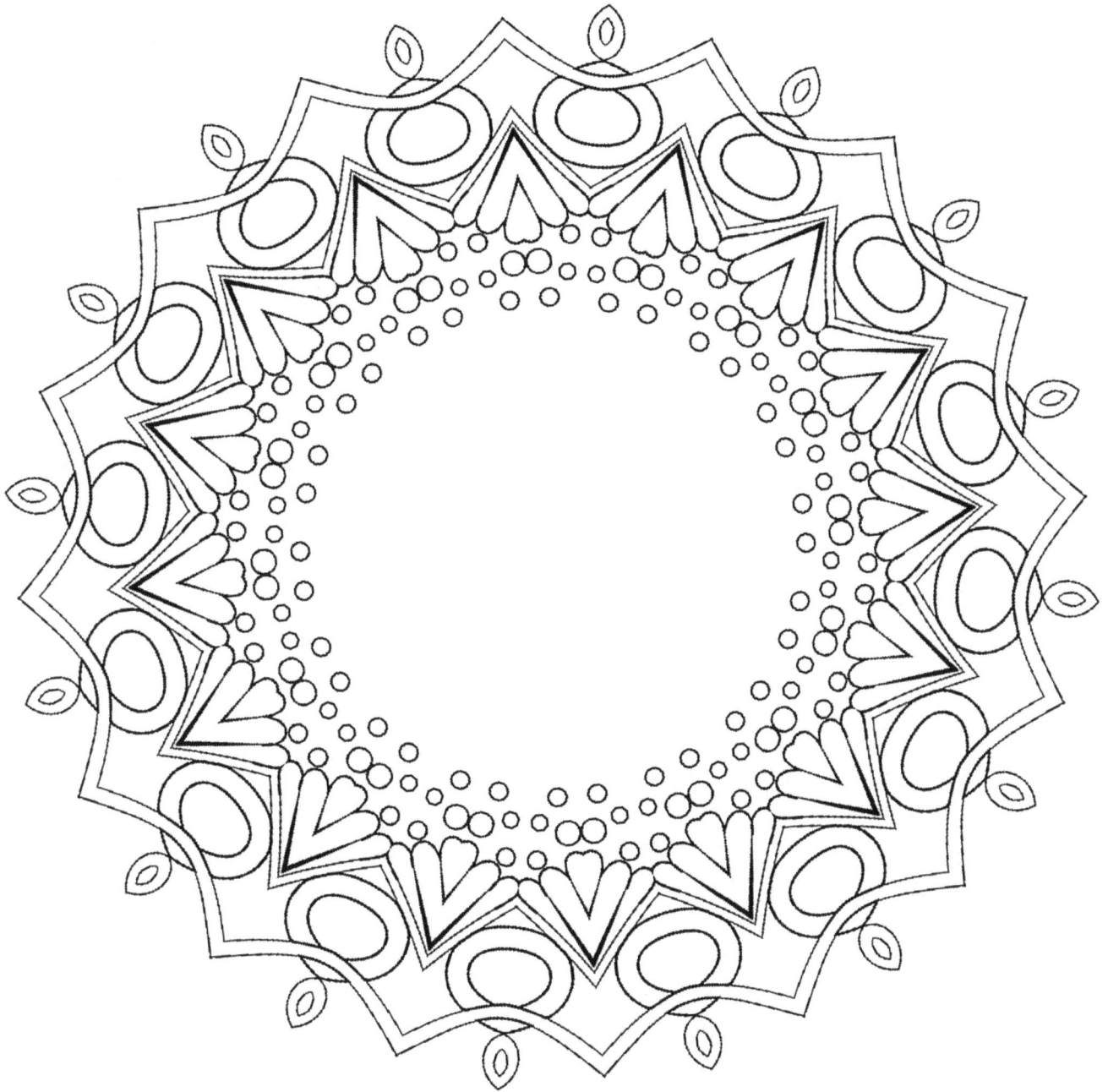

The best and most beautiful things in this world
cannot be seen or even heard,
but must be felt with the heart.
- Helen Keller

You know you're in love
when you don't want to fall asleep
because reality is finally better than your dreams.
- Dr. Seuss

Lots of people want to ride with you in the limo,
but what you want is someone
who will take the bus with you
when the limo breaks down.
- Oprah Winfrey

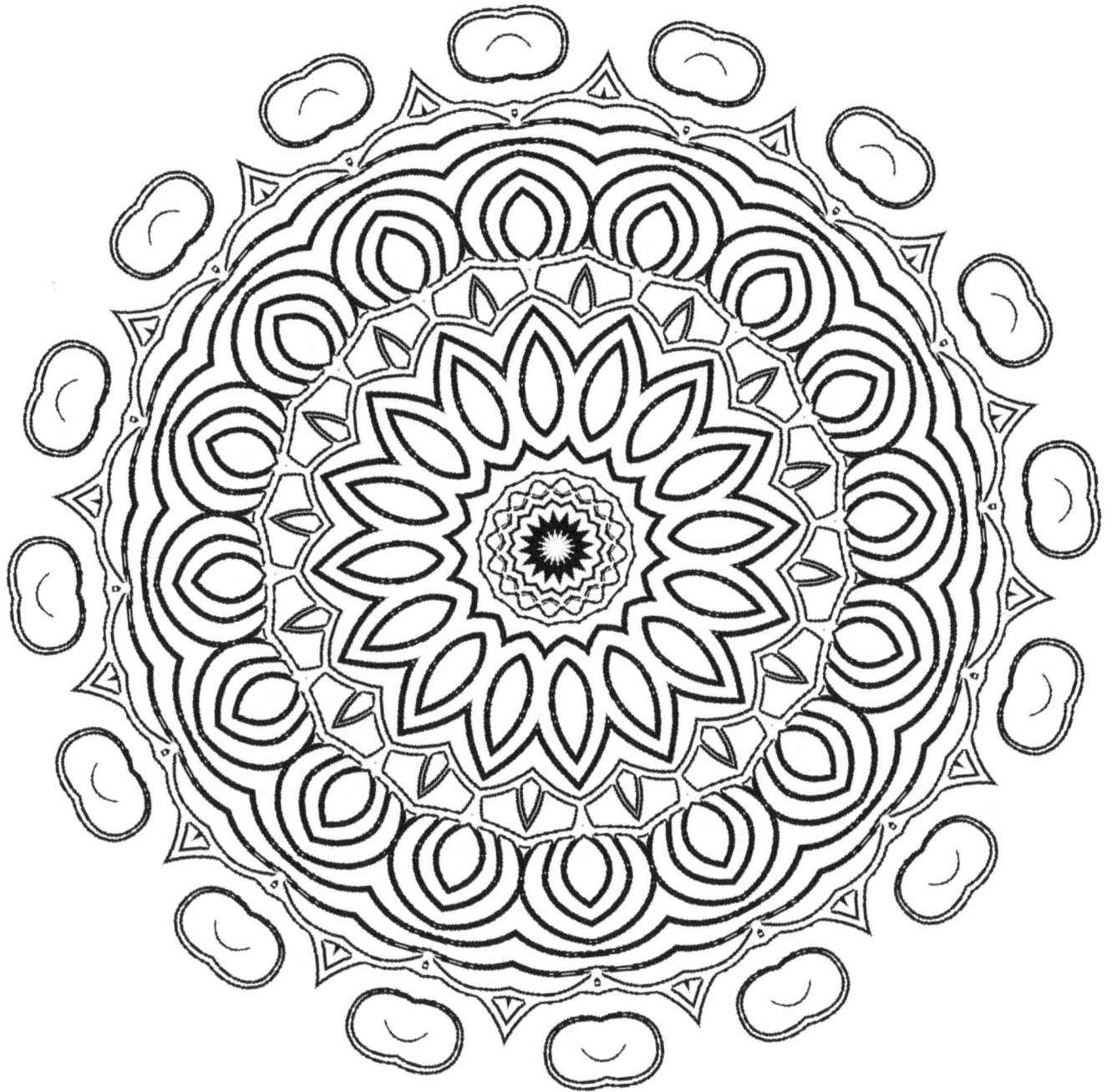

'Tis better to have loved and lost
than never to have loved at all.
- Alfred Lord Tennyson

I have decided to stick with love.
Hate is too great a burden to bear.
- Martin Luther King, Jr.

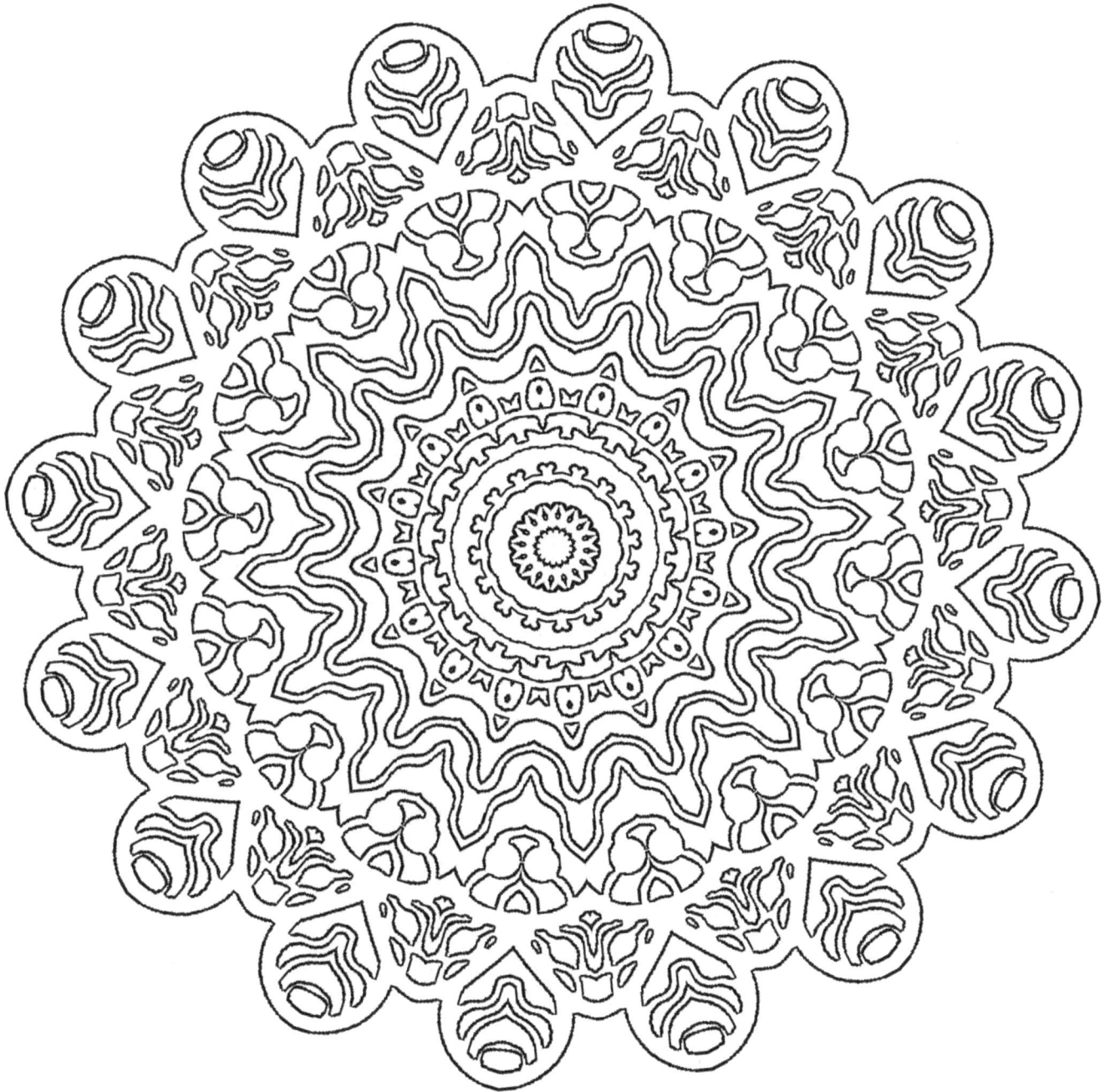

I love you without knowing how, or when, or from where.
I love you straightforwardly, without complexities or pride;
so I love you because I know no other way.
- Pablo Neruda

Twenty years from now you will be more disappointed
by the things that you didn't do than by the ones you did do.
So throw off the bowlines.
Catch the trade winds in your sails.
Explore. Dream. Discover.
- Mark Twain

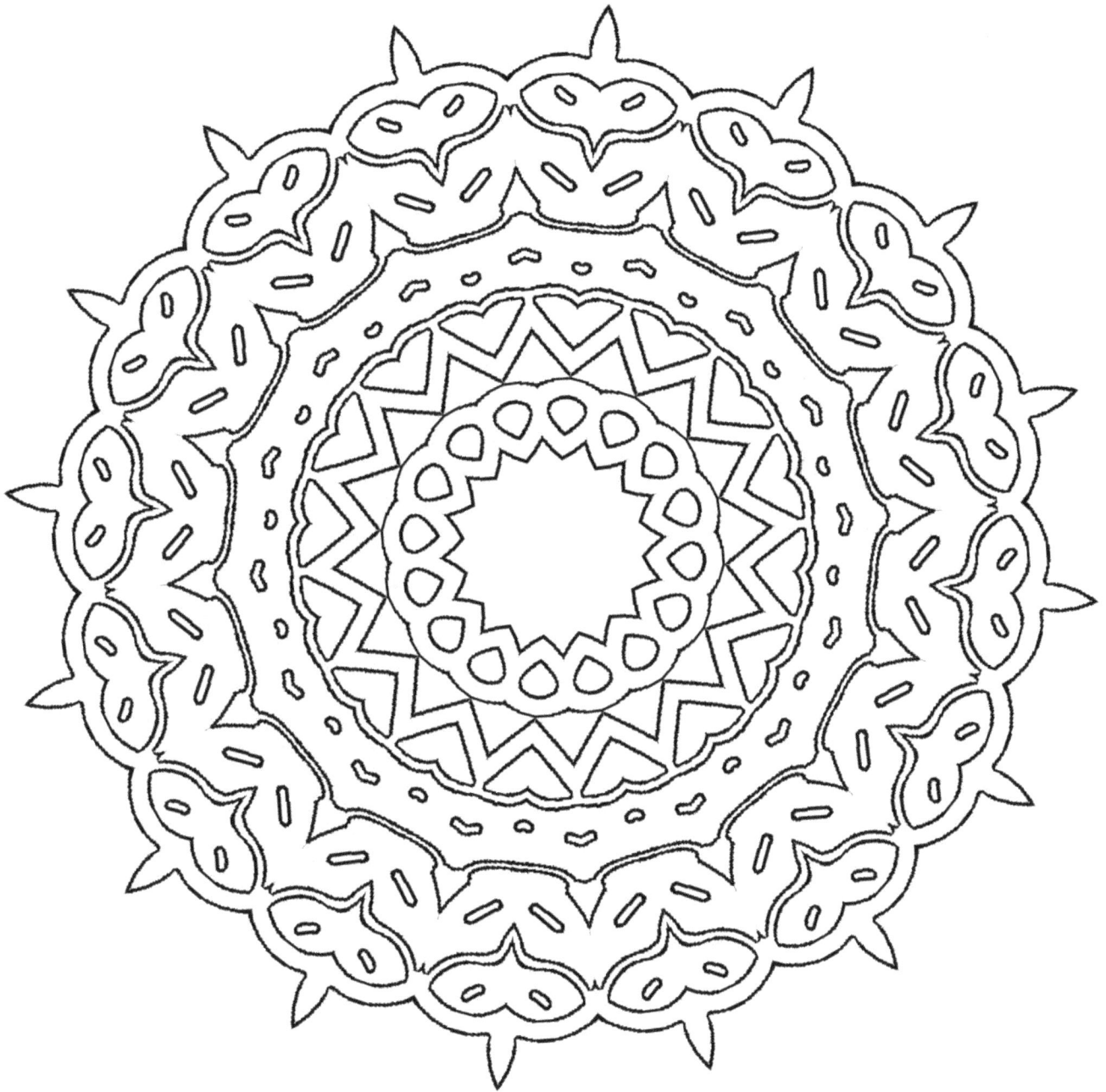

I have found that if you love life, life will love you back.
- Arthur Rubinstein

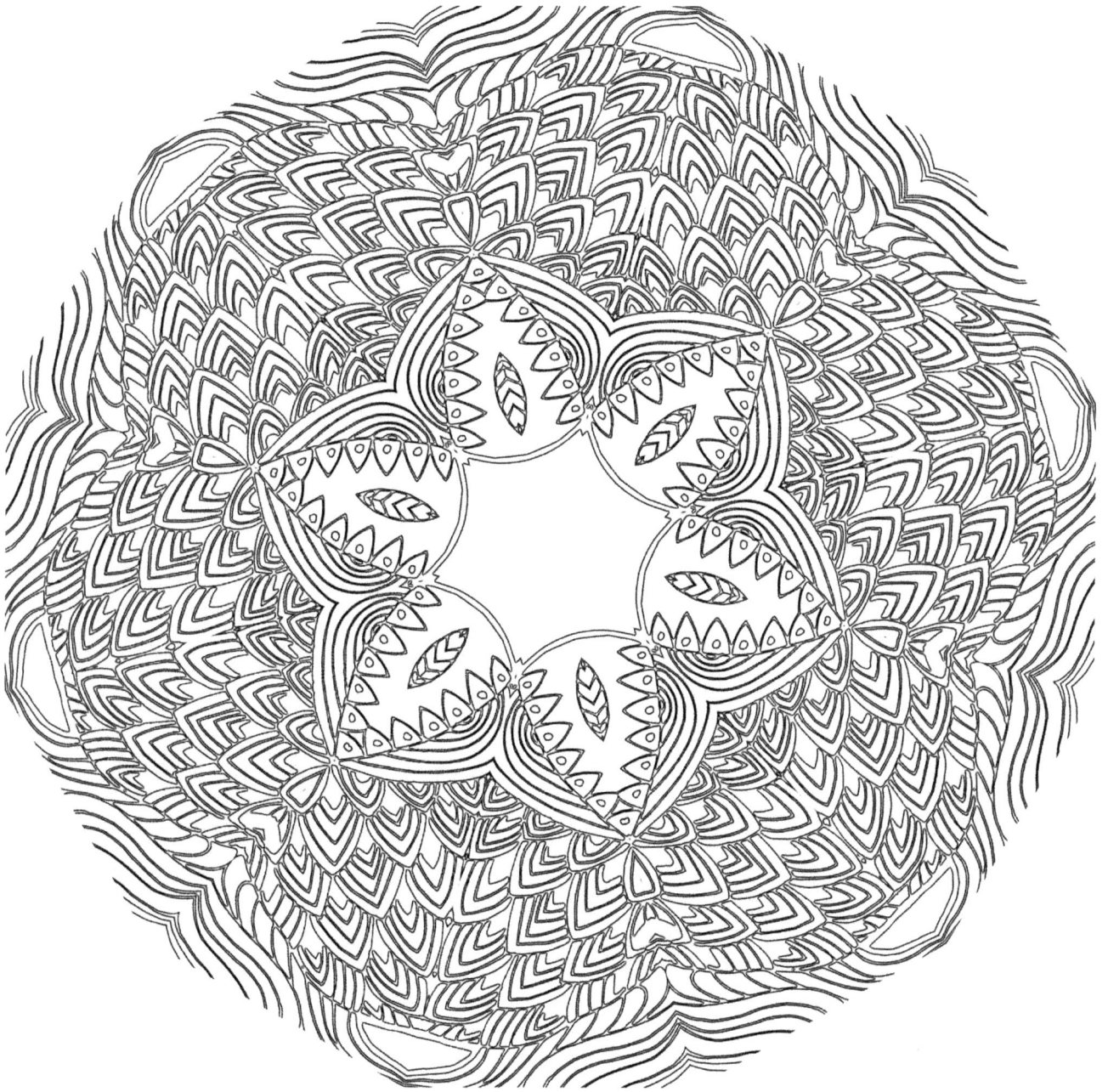

There are two ways to live your life.
One is as though nothing is a miracle.
The other is as though everything is a miracle
- Albert Einstein

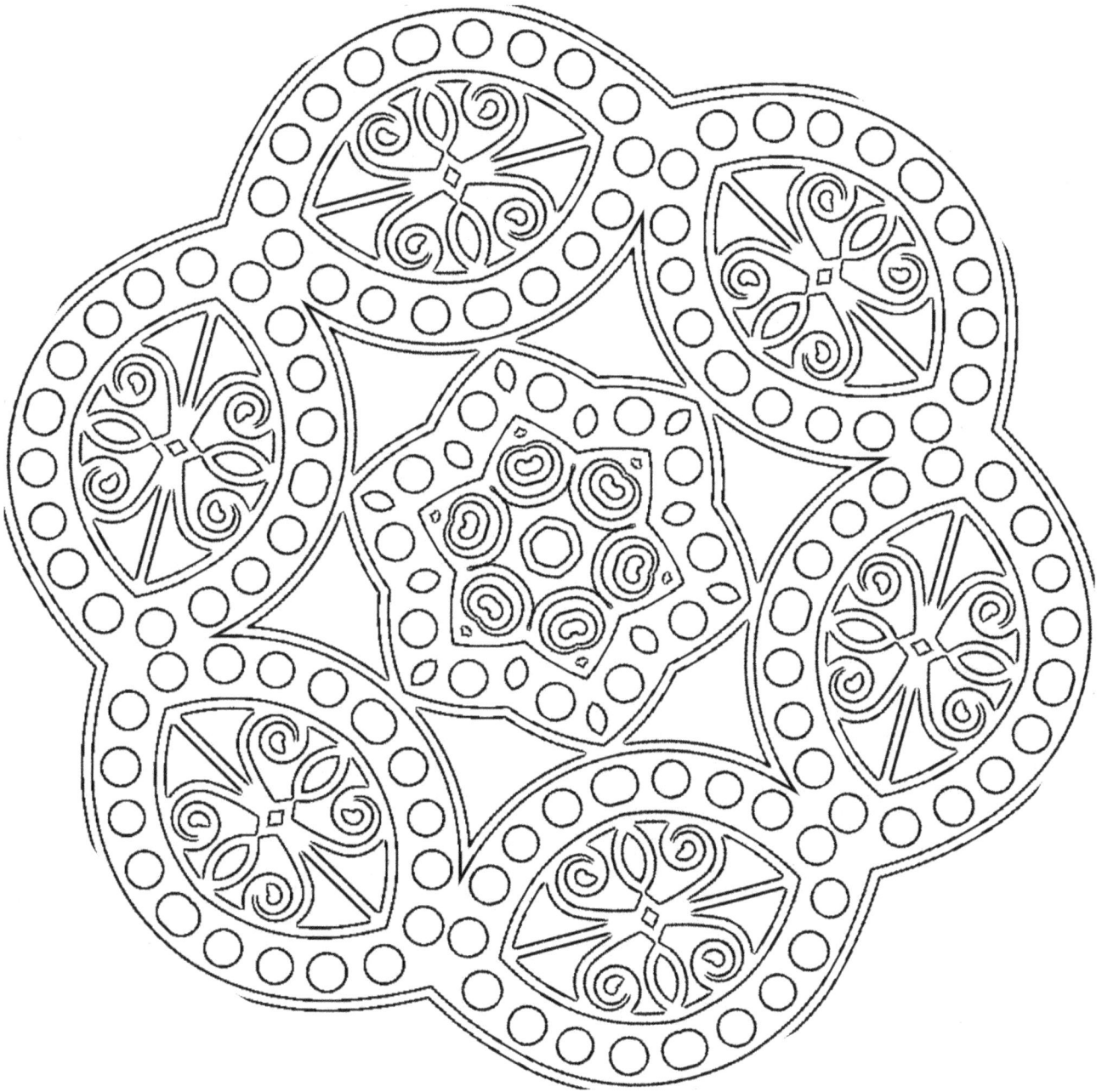

In the end, it's not going to matter how many breaths you took, but how many moments took your breath away
- Shing Xiong

Love does not come to those who seek it,
but to those who give love.
It is a binding force between souls
who have nothing to give
but themselves to one another.
- Harold Clemp

To have and to hold,
from this day forward,
for better, for worse,
for richer, for poorer,
in sickness and in health,
until death do us part.
- Book of Common Prayer

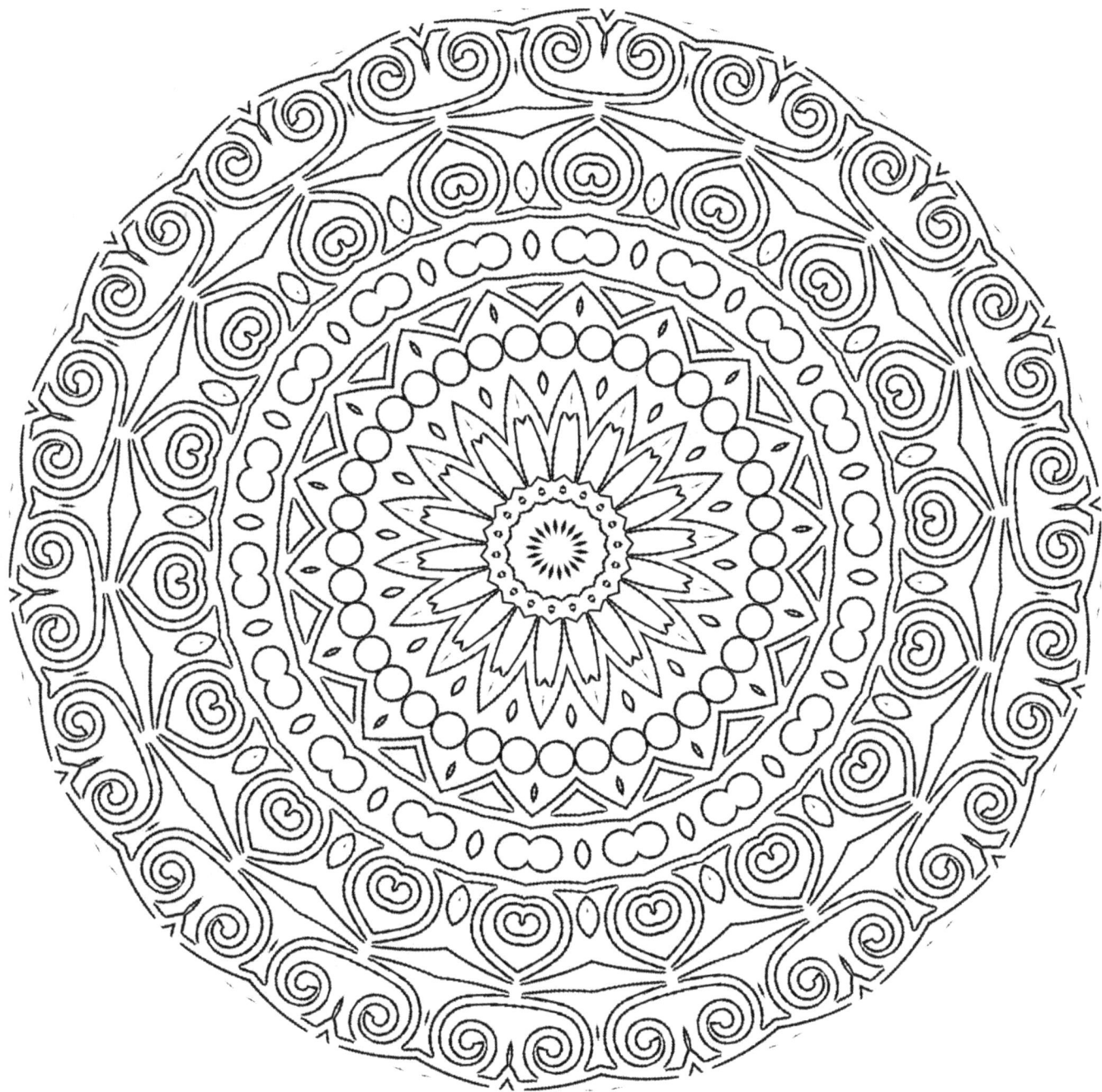

I have found the paradox,
that if you love until it hurts,
there can be no more hurt,
only more love.
- Mother Teresa

The best thing to hold onto in life is each other.
- Audrey Hepburn

Love is life. And if you miss love, you miss life.
- Leo Buscaglia

Spread love everywhere you go.
Let no one ever come to you without leaving happier.
- Mother Teresa

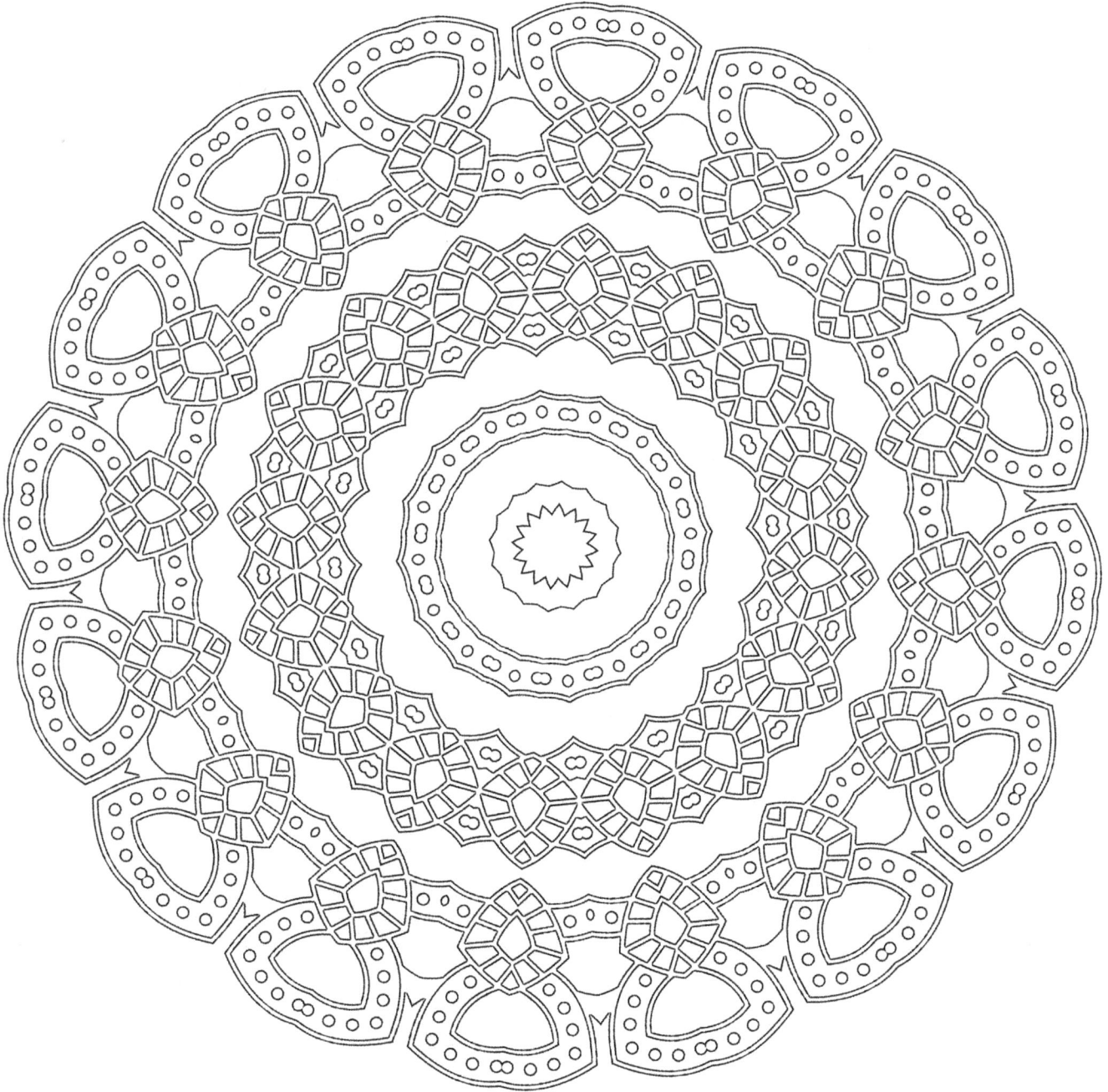

The course of true love never did run smooth.
- William Shakespeare

Treasure the love you receive above all.
It will survive long after
your good health has vanished.
– Og Mandino

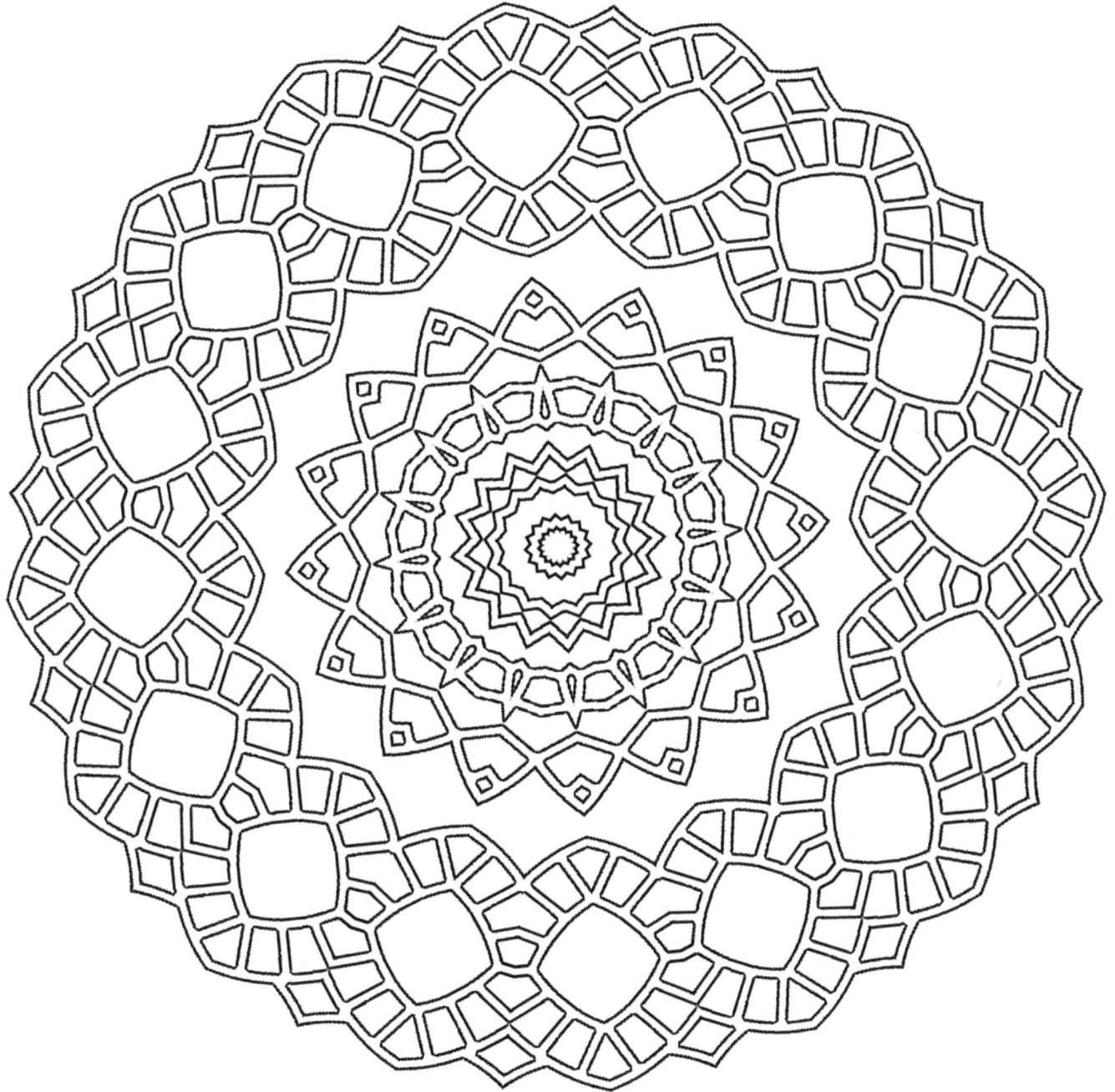

Love looks not with the eyes,
but with the mind,
And therefore is winged Cupid painted blind.
- William Shakespeare

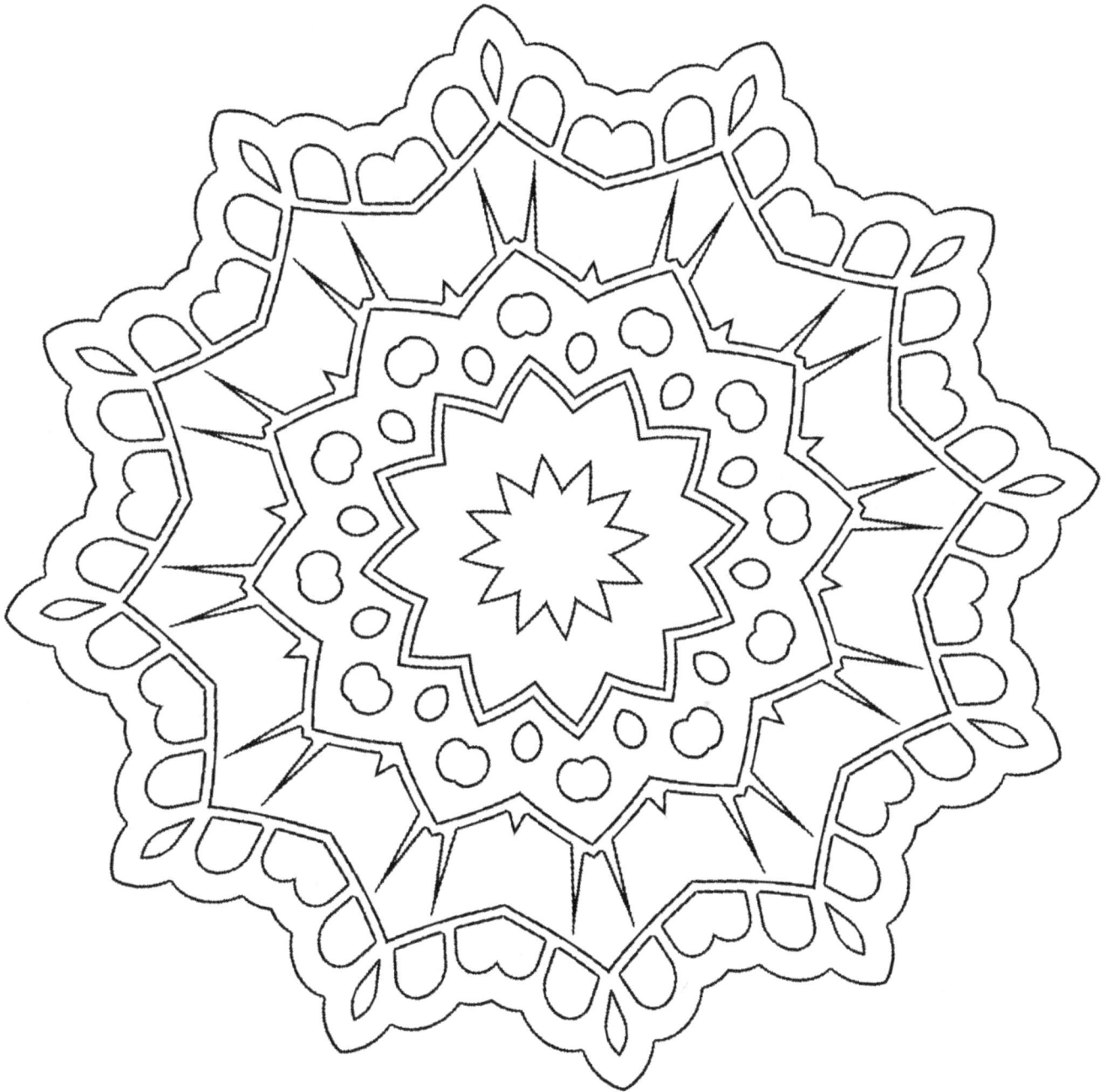

Lord, make me an instrument of thy peace.
Where there is hatred, let me sow love.
- Francis of Assisi

Love recognizes no barriers.
It jumps hurdles,
leaps fences,
penetrates walls
to arrive at its destination full of hope.
- Maya Angelou

Since love grows within you,
so beauty grows.
For love is the beauty of the soul.
- Saint Augustine

Love begins at home,
and it is not how much we do...
but how much love we put in that action.
- Mother Teresa

The greatest healing therapy is friendship and love.
- Hubert H. Humphrey

Intense love does not measure, it just gives.
– Mother Teresa

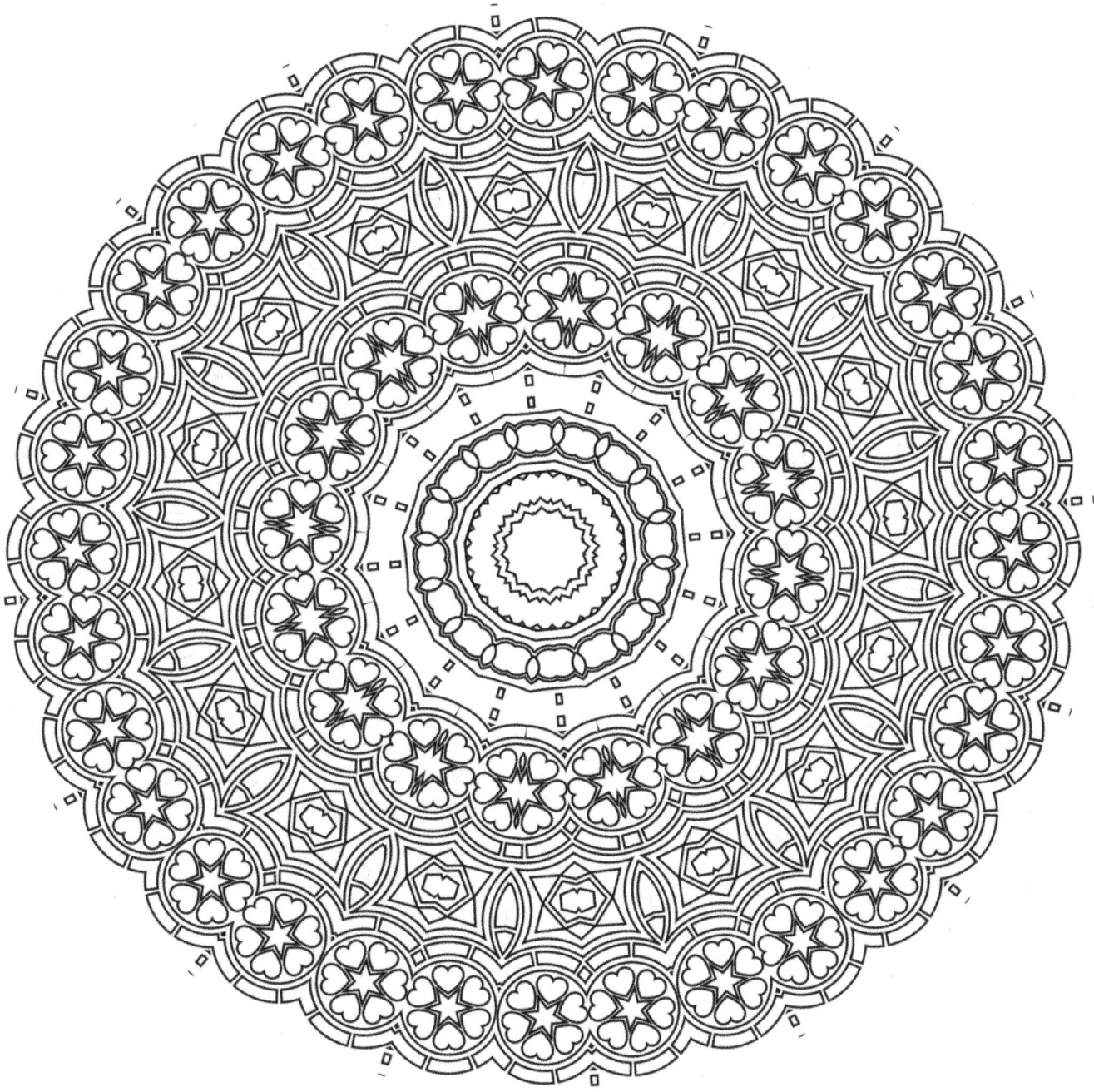

Love is the only force
capable of transforming an enemy into friend.
- Martin Luther King, Jr.

Choose a job you love,
and you will never have to work
a day in your life.
- Confucius

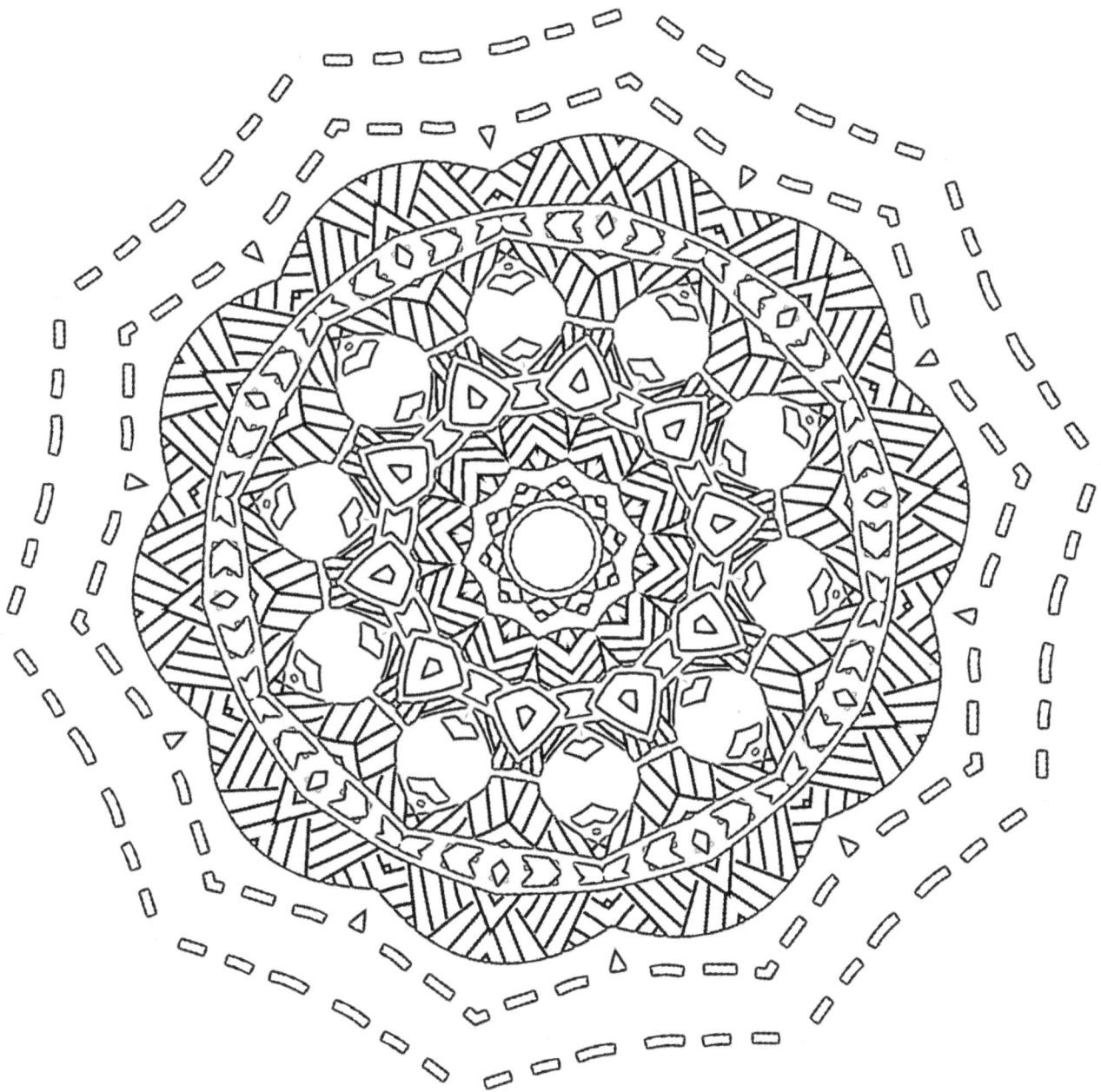

Your work is going to fill a large part of your life,
and the only way to be truly satisfied
is to do what you believe is great work.
And the only way to do great work
is to love what you do.
If you haven't found it yet, keep looking.
Don't settle.
As with all matters of the heart,
you'll know when you find it.
- Steve Jobs

For love is immortality.
- Emily Dickinson

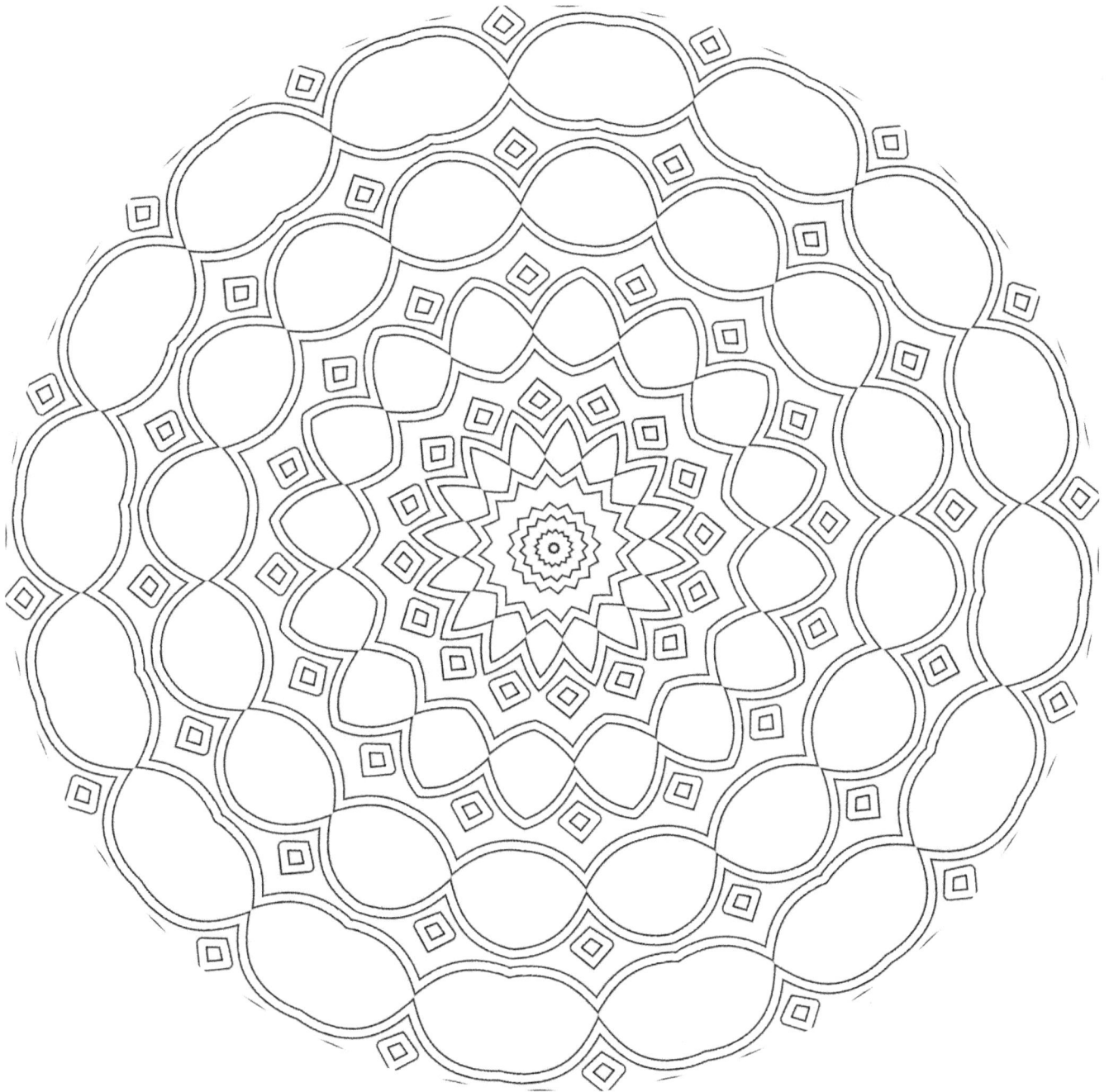

Accustom yourself continually
to make many acts of love,
for they enkindle and melt the soul.
- Saint Teresa of Avila

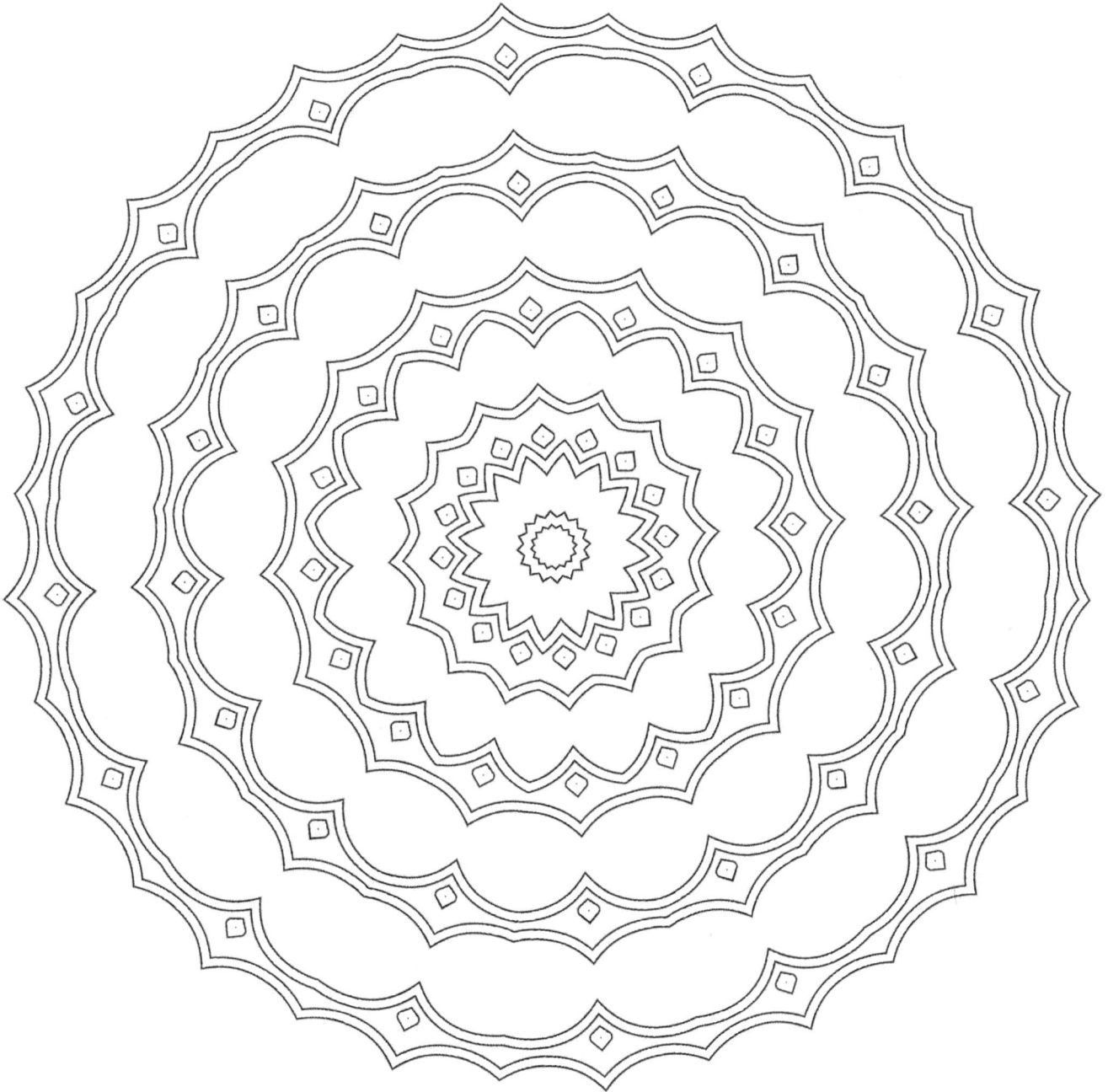

The cure for all the ills and wrongs,
the cares, the sorrows,
and the crimes of humanity,
all lie in the one word 'love'.
It is the divine vitality
that everywhere produces and restores life.
- Lydia M. Child

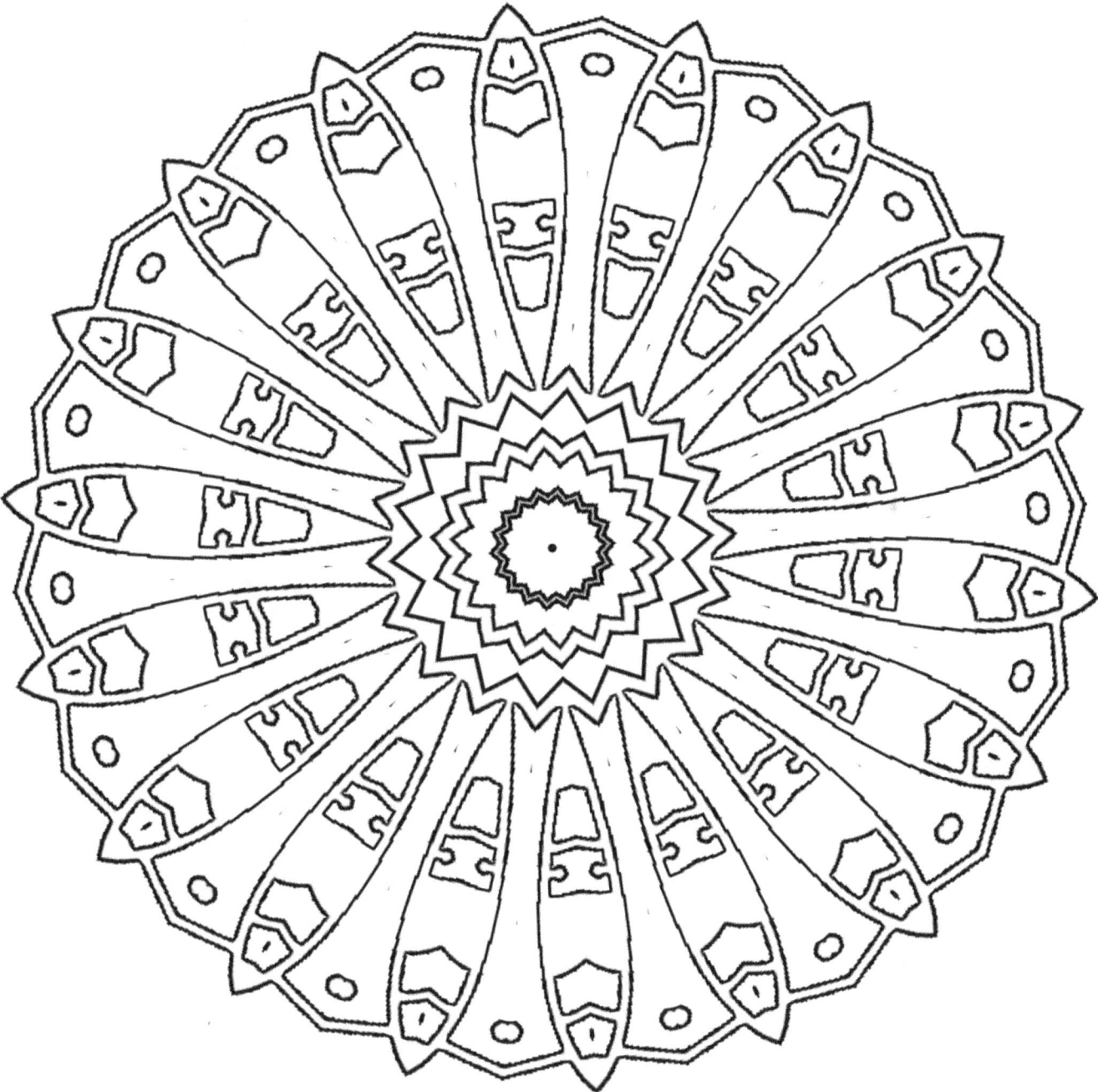

There is room in the smallest cottage for a happy loving pair.
- Friedrich Schiller

Come live in my heart, and pay no rent.
- Samuel Lover

Let no one who loves be unhappy,
even love unreturned has its rainbow.
- James M. Barrie

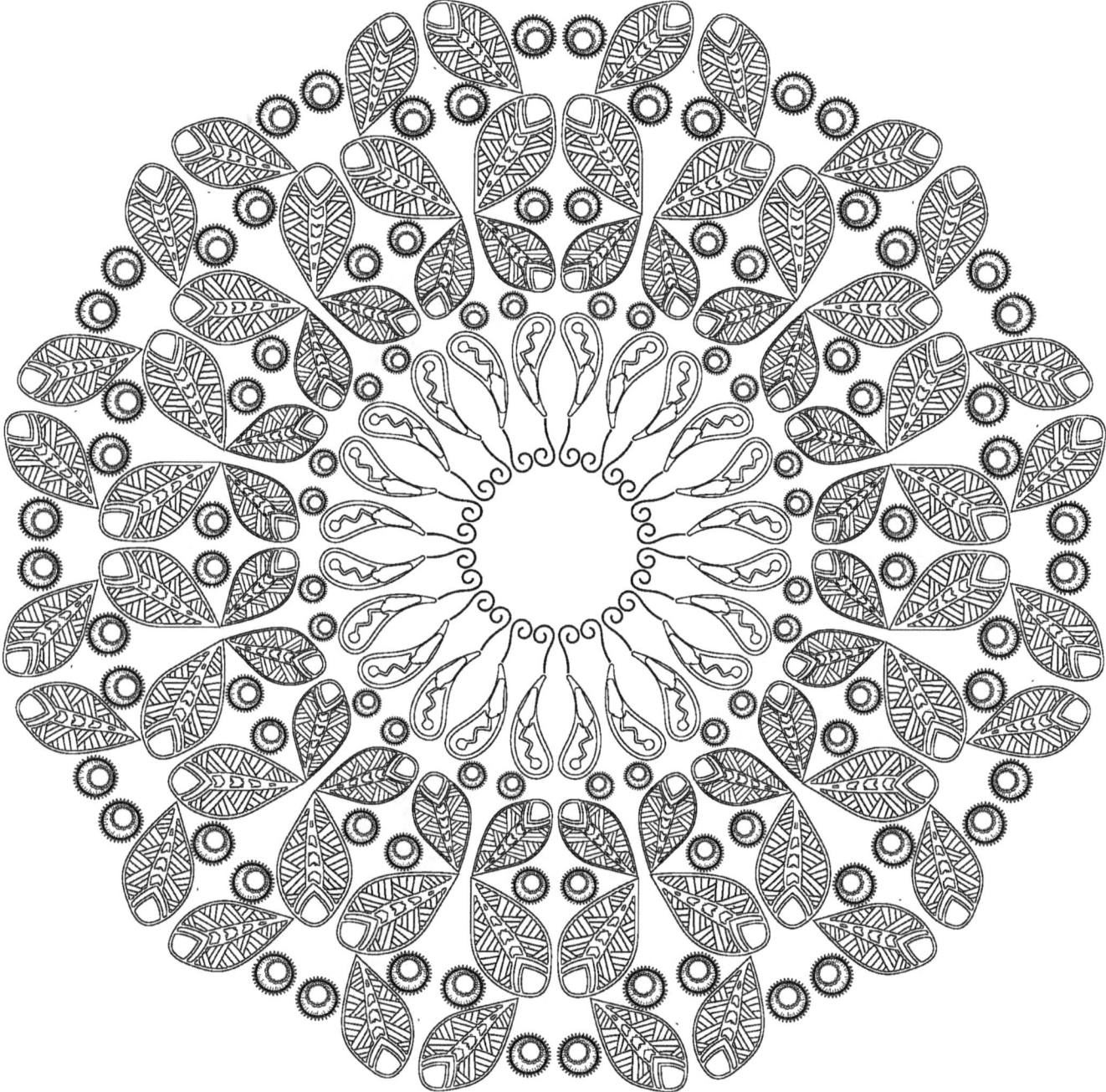

Love is always bestowed as a gift -
freely, willingly and without expectation.
We don't love to be loved; we love to love.
– Leo Buscaglia

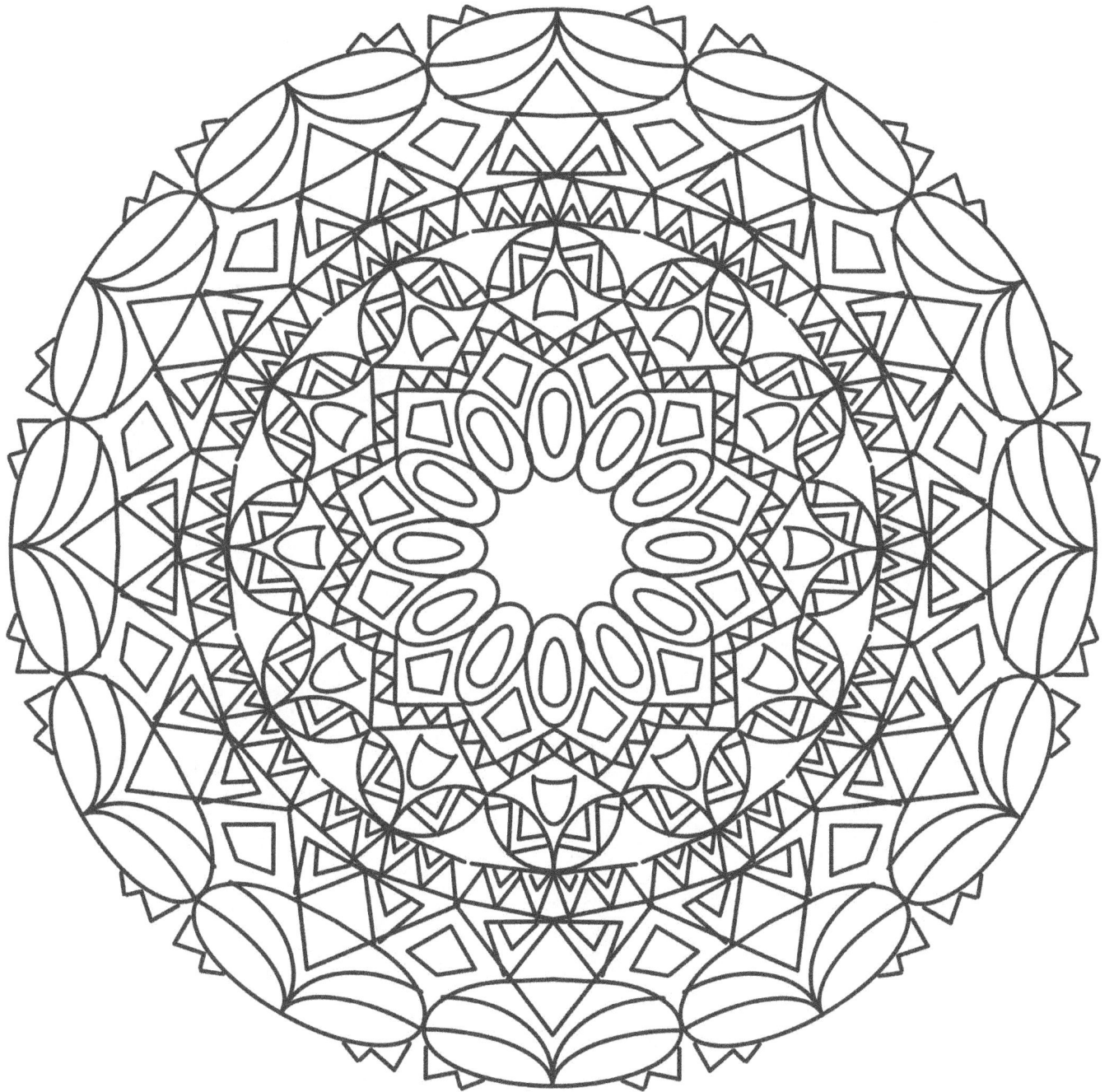

Love is a canvas furnished by nature
and embroidered by imagination.
- Voltaire

In our life there is a single color,
as on an artist's palette,
which provides the meaning of life and art.
It is the color of love.
- Marc Chagall

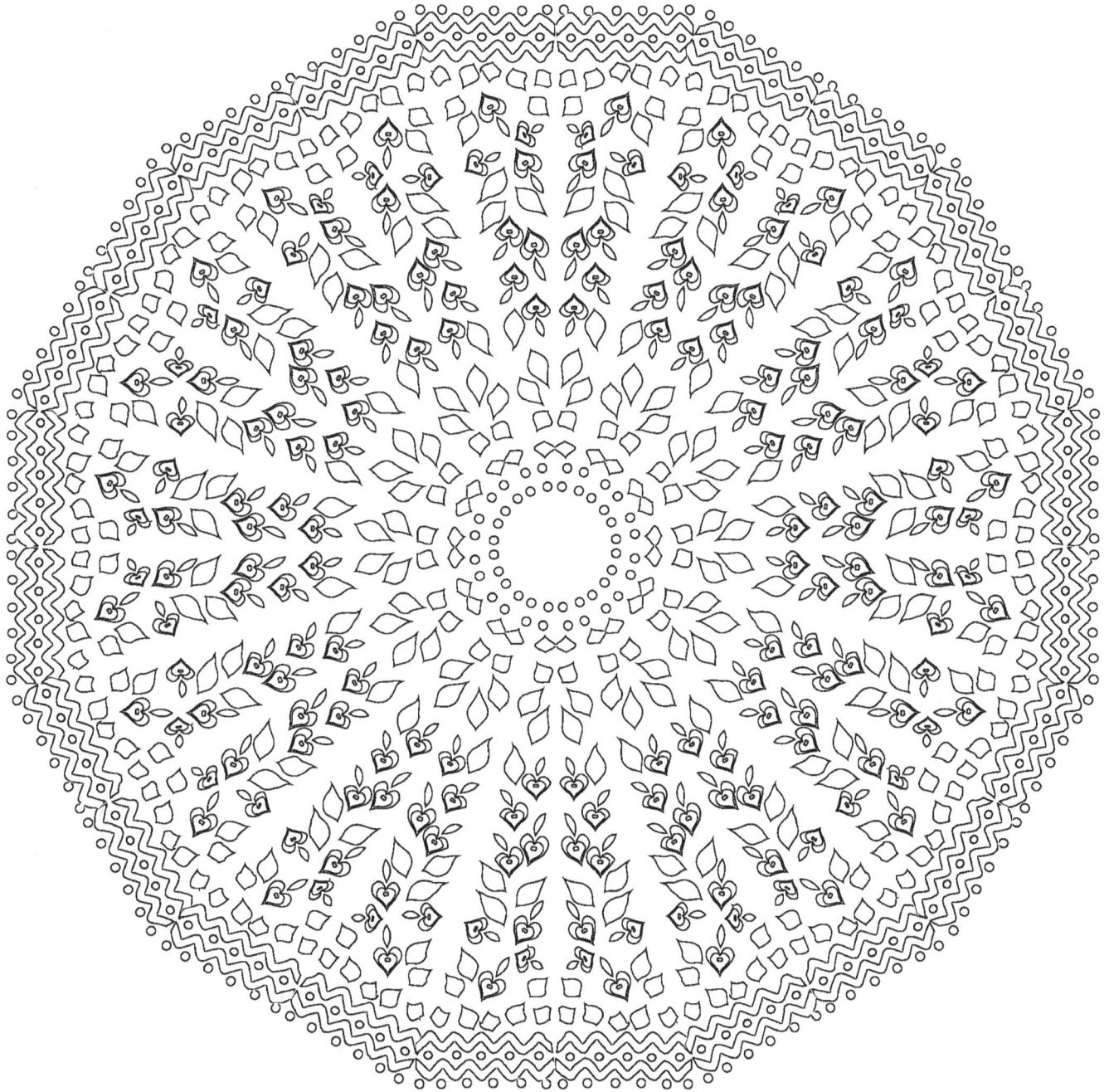

Love does not consist in gazing at each other,
but in looking outward together
in the same direction.
- Antoine de Saint-Exupery

As the Father has loved me, so have I loved you.
- Jesus Christ

Do all things with love.
- Og Mandino

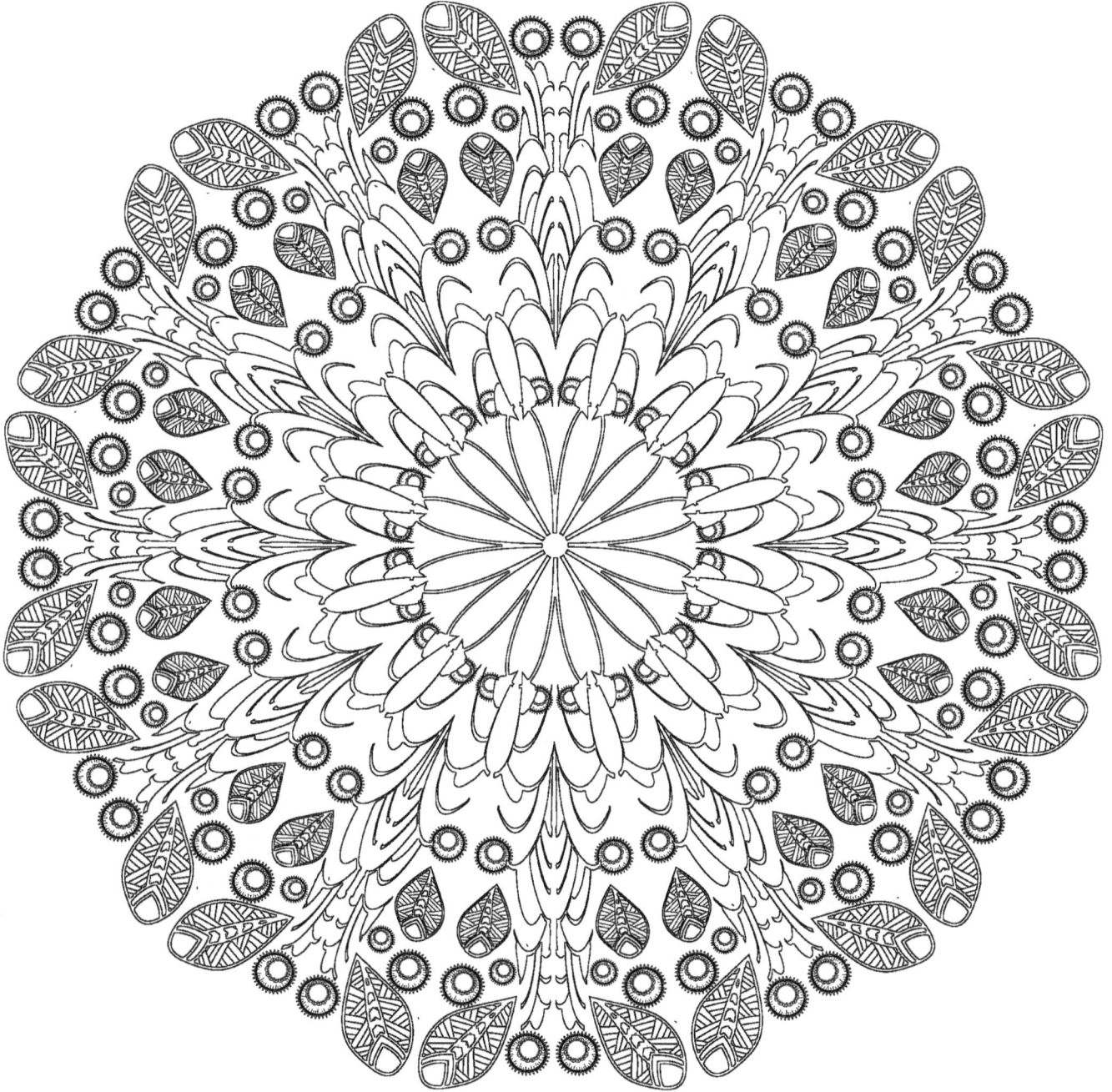

Love means not ever having to say you're sorry.
- Erich Segal

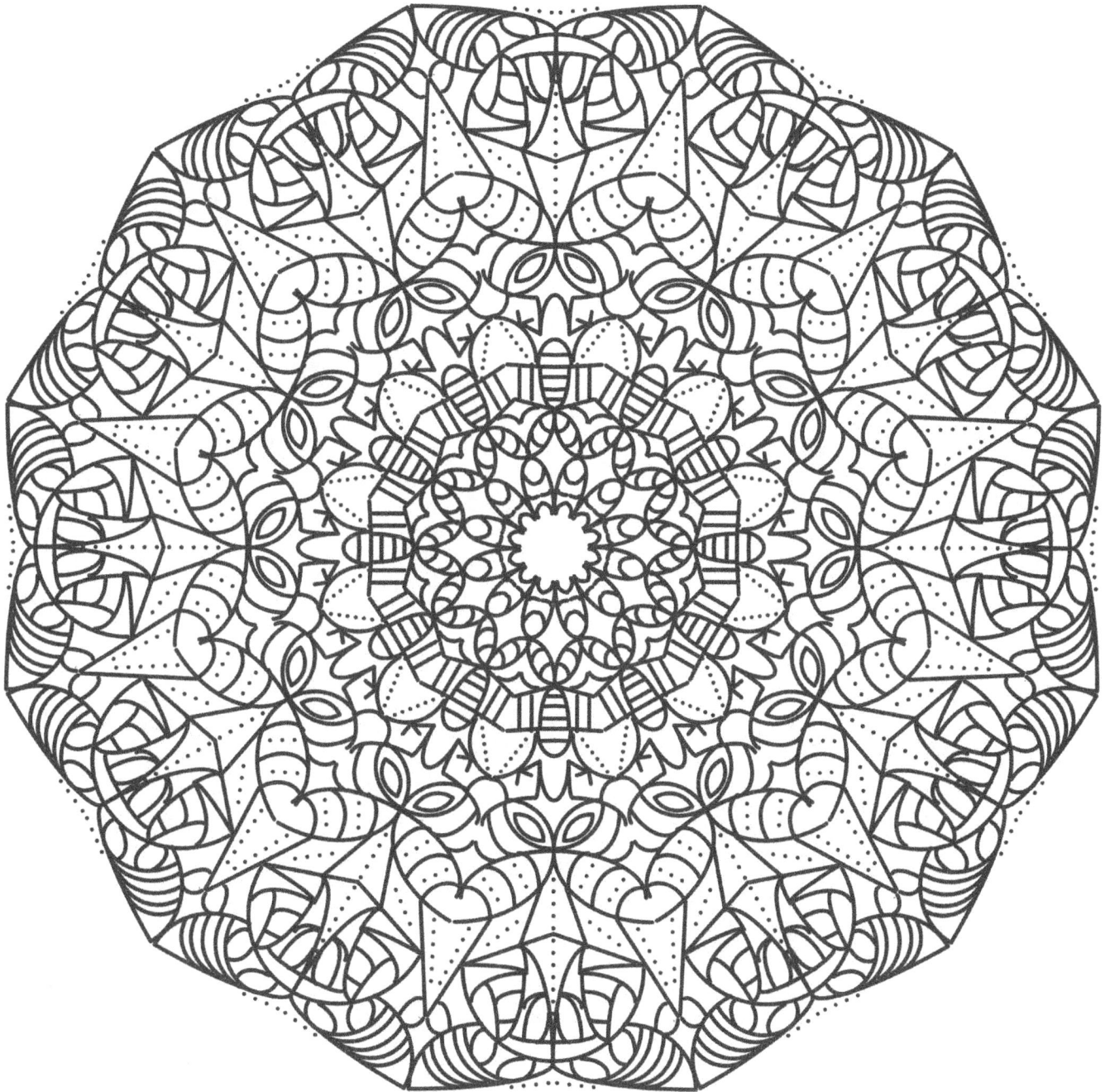

Don't walk in front of me,
I may not follow.
Don't walk behind me,
I may not lead.
There is only one happiness in life,
to love and be loved.
        - George Sand

You learn to speak by speaking,
to study by studying,
to run by running,
to work by working;
in just the same way,
you learn to love by loving.
- Anatole France

English - I love you
Mandarin - Wo ai ni
Filipino - Mahal kita
French - Je t'aime, Je t'adore
German - Ich liebe dich
Hawaiian - Aloha Au Ia`oe
Italian - Ti amo
Japanese - Aishiteru or Anata ga daisuki desu
Korean - Sarang Heyo or Nanun tangshinul sarang hamnida
Japanese - Aishiteru or Anata ga daisuki desu
Russian - Ya tebya liubliu
Spanish - Te quiero / Te amo
Taiwanese - Wa ga ei li
Thai - Phom rak khun

Love conquers all.
- Virgil

©K.S. Pierce, www.coloringbooklove.com

Love is patient, love is kind.
It does not envy,
it does not boast, it is not proud.
It does not dishonor others,
it is not self-seeking,
it is not easily angered,
it keeps no record of wrongs.
Love does not delight in evil
but rejoices with the truth.
It always protects, always trusts,
always hopes, always perseveres.
Love never fails.

- 1 Corinthians 13:4-8

SHARE YOUR CREATIONS WITH US!

www.ingramcontent.com/pod-product-compliance
Lightning Source LLC
Chambersburg PA
CBHW080935040426
42443CB00015B/3426